THIS IS

2020

part two

KASSIE J RUNYAN

Library of Congress Cataloging Data
Library of Congress Control Number: 2021909154

ISBN (paperback): 9781735514048
ISBN (ebook): 9781735514055

DEDICATION

Part one was dedicated to the heroes of the year and we still cannot recognize or thank them enough- even as we stopped clapping- you are still the magic that keep the human race going. We thank you.

Part two is dedicated to the people who were lost in 2020 and 2021. Take a moment to think of the holes left in our lives. To the friends and neighbors that I've lost in the past year. Ones that will forever be seared in my heart and mind as they left us too soon. In one breath I am excited for a 'return to normal' when I can head to the local park and spend my Saturday mornings writing there- typing broken by the short conversations with the regulars who became friends over five years. The next breath makes me dread the same moment- knowing the faces that will no longer show up with a smile. My words and my love are dedicated to them and to those lost around the world to a disease that we could not and can not deny or hide from.

FORWARD

Mr. Rogers once said "Look for the helpers. You will always find people who are helping."

It is a great piece of advice. When the world is breaking, and you don't know where to look or who to turn to. When you feel that there is no way for the world to get better... look for the helpers.

However, we are no longer the children looking for help. We have now grown into capable adults and it is time to challenge ourselves to do more. We need to strive to be the helpers that others look for. Only we can make a difference in this world.

Become the helper.

PART ONE

Part one of "This is 2020" came out in July of 2021. It was originally expected to be the only part and was written live in each month as I was overwhelmed with anxiety from Covid, anger towards people outside NY not seeing the temporary morgue truck down the block from us and not believing what was going on, confusion and then incensed about the ongoing systematic racism across the US and beyond. I have written poetry for years but this was the first time I was consistently writing and sharing it to social media and it took off. The decision was made to publish the collection as a way to provide additional donations to two wonderful organizations- something that I could do for action while staying safe in my home. After the success of Part One, and requests for a book to finish out the year, I decided to make Part Two. Part Two takes a bit of a different approach but still follows the year and each poem was written in the moment and within the month it's placed.

You can find Part One at KassieJRunyan.com, IndieBound.org, Amazon, Barnes & Noble, and other major bookstores.

July

MAN IN THE MIRROR

you stand there

staring at the eyes

that look a bit like yours

as they stare back at you.

do you still recognize their hue?

and the slant of their lids?

the wrinkles have grown deeper.

there is sadness there;

some call it wisdom.

you haven't made the world better.

not like you promised.

there is still time

but the eyes look doubtful

and the lines give away the fallen years.

stop.

you aren't yet dead.

recognition grows in the eyes

of the man staring back at you

as you stand up straighter

reminded that the change you promised;

it starts with you.

wrinkles be damned.

there's still time

to make a change.

the eyes grow bright

and for the first time

in a long time

you recognize the person behind the eyes.

you smile at this man in the mirror

before turning to the door

to meet the new day.

AS I LAY DYING

as I lay dying

will I know I'm declining

or expiring?

will they be crying

and denying?

a priest occupying

and purifying

ignoring my defying.

was my life satisfying

or mystifying?

did I do enough applying

or complying

or flat out buying?

was I disqualifying

in my intensifying

need for personifying

and verifying

and gratifying

and overflying?

will I be able to stop trying

and only focus on flying

as I leave my body behind?

CONVERSATION

let's have a conversation

longer than a quick chat

we'll have ourselves a moment

and enjoy it at that

we'll talk of mountains oh so high

and valleys way down low

of stars and suns and moons so bright

our imagination will grow

we'll remember the places of yesterday

and plan seeing them again

planes and trains and ships, oh my

how will we ever abstain

I can't wait until I've got my shot

and I'll jump right out the door

to see all of the things I've missed

that I just can't wait to explore

VOICES INSIDE MY HEAD

help would

be emptied

by others

taken and pushed

lopsided in anger

now friends drift further

and enemies shout

from inside

my own head

they tap

tap

tap

against my skull

trying to get out

into the world

shouting and snarling.

the friends

used to quiet them

hush them into

submission

those friends now gone

and the voices run wild

in charge of the narrative

clenching my teeth

and squeezing my eyes

to keep the voices inside

I breathe in

and out

and the voices

start to calm

to only a dull

roar

FIND THE GOOD

in every tragedy there is good, if you only know where to look

the moms providing school supplies to children in need

the doctors working tirelessly without sleep or rest

when I was a kid, I remember being told that if

"you don't have anything nice to say, don't

say anything at all." why has this rule

disappeared with the times? the

trolls commenting on news

stories could learn from

that. this is the

time to hope

and fight

and

learn.

to do better.

to be better. a

lesson for us all. we

need to be like the good

that we see in the world if we

only stop to look around. the gangs

distributing food to those in need. people

stopping to defend a stranger on the street.

this is the world that I wish to see. the world that

is worth fighting for. we need to find the joy in helping

others again. it shouldn't be that difficult. we already know

what we need to do. we need to **stand up and become the helpers**.

OH, MOTHER EARTH

I suckle at her breast

trying not to wake her

the sleeping woman, dressed in white

innocent of heartache and heartbreak

hopeful dreams visioning

the future that has yet to come

a future of growth and hope

that could yet come to be

she smiles in her sleep

and her hand caresses my small head

mother and child

alone in peace

I suckle at her breast

growing full

in a building desperation

to take the milk she has given

she stirs, her eyes

fluttering open

and confusion

wrinkles her brow

as her dress dyes

from white to green

her nipple is torn

from my lips

my body pulled back

by another child

a child like me

but different

I watch as he

lunges towards her breast

and she feeds him

without hesitation

jealousy climbing my body

putting my skin to tingle

my full belly replaced by the

hunger of envy

he suckles at her breast

as I'm pushed away further

the dizziness building

as I'm turning and swirling

through the throngs of children

eagerly waiting their turn

numbers growing

building

doubling

by each and every second

their voices

growing louder

as their patience wanes

I stand on the tips of my toes

neck straining

trying to see her

but gaining only a glimpse

of her arms

held in place

by her side

and the ripped sleeve of

her dress turned red

the torn edge of silk held up

above the crowd

by a dirty hand

and the crowd cheers

and jeers.

their ownership desire unchecked

I'm picked up by the wave

of pushing and pulsating bodies

trying to get closer

to the single source

of nourishment

but I fall to the ground

and peer through the legs

finally seeing her face again

strained with pain and

devastation

and again confusion

small hands reaching to her

pawing at her

clawing at her

worshiping her and the boys

standing at the front

of the line

who in turn

bow to the children

attached to each nipple

they hungrily suckle at her breast

as the shouts grow

louder above me

and I look up

to see a fist land

on a soft cheek

eyes growing red as the faces

erupt in angst

I roll along the

ground, avoiding the stomping feet

I slither towards where I know she lays

telling myself I will save her

from these power hungry children

fighting over her

no, I

don't want to own her

for myself

how could you even ask that?

I giggle as my mouth waters

craving her milk

the fight rampages above

but *I'm* not angry like *them*

and I lack that obsessive need

I crawl quicker seeing a glimpse

of her limp leg

shrouded in deep black cloth

"oh, mother"

I howl

"please don't forsake us!

how can we show you

that we still adore you?"

I get to an opening and stand

ducking quickly below a bullet

fired from a found gun

and held in the hand

of a boy

not aiming for me

I run towards her body

as an explosion shakes

the ground behind me

no one is suckling at her breast

by the time I make it to her side

to see her laying there

now abandoned and naked

not able to pull

the last shred of the dull grey

fabric to cover herself

as the battle rages behind me

I move my mouth to her flattened breast

and pull

trying to get just one more

drip...

but nothing comes

I release her breast and raise

my head to the sky

an anguished cry

escaping my lips

"oh, mother

why have *YOU* forsaken *US?*

we *ONLY* wanted to love you"

AUGUST

LILY

my cat is dependent on zoom

when I start a call, she sprints into the room

hitting my chair with a loud boom

as she maneuvers her tail to the screen,

I try to move my head in between

them just before she starts to preen

bending to show everyone her flexibility

tucking her head to prove her agility

waiting for the vocal gullibility

as everyone laughs and coos

making me take a moment to introduce

and she stretches and shows her caboose

this lasts for the full call

sometimes around my chair she'll crawl

and look longingly at my coworker, Paul

everyone says goodbye (to Lily not me)

making me feel almost absentee

just before she prances away, carefree

MASKS

twelve faces

ten masks

three noses uncovered

too much skin

too much breath

wheezing as they walk by

coughing into the open sky

it should be so simple

cover you mouth and nose

the children do it without reprise

the fear doesn't show in their eyes

what am I missing

why is it so difficult

so that in a month

there aren't

four ventilated grimaces

and a body bag

I'M THE LUCKY ONE

in a family with a history

I was born to the mom

that shed

her family's past

and fought for a better life.

I'm the lucky one.

in a small house

in a small town

I was raised without need

and with a love

from a father who sacrificed

so we could have extra.

I'm the lucky one.

with a varied history

over my years

and a troubled past

full of troubled people

making troubling decisions

and fearful nights

but here I am now

as I look around.

I'm the lucky one.

with a body

that doesn't cooperate

or coordinate

or function as it should.

I have family enough

and beautiful girls

turning into smart women

who call me auntie.

I'm the lucky one.

in a world where people want

and need

and struggle

here is my job

in a place I respect

with people who are family.

I'm the lucky one.

I can explore the world

no longer just in books

see the mountains

feel the sea breeze

follow the paths of my heroes

in awe with each flight

and each step.

I'm the lucky one.

in a world that is unjust

and forced leaders that

have abandoned those in need

while pushing others

to the ground

because those they think are below

do not look

or love

like the rulers do.

I'm the lucky one.

as disease ravages the world

and blocks the air

in the chests of the people

struggling for breath

and for life

I cower in my home

protected by glass

hugging my chest to

protect my lungs

that were scarred years before

but here...

I am the lucky one.

WHERE IS THE BLUE LINE

"back the blue"

the crowd chants on queue

without seeing the clue

that "back the blue"

impacts more than a few

also negative for those who

wear the uniform of blue

they are asked to be the crew

to do what they shouldn't have to do

issues with funding pull through

yet a crowd yells "back the blue"

just as they were told to do

and we keep having deja vu

that impacts those with a skin hue

it's time to spread what is due

expanding our field of view

and quit screaming "back the blue"

DARKNESS

a creature

ragged and broken

whose kingdom remained

stripped of the

daylight

IMPOSTOR SYNDROME

do they see me working

from behind the screen

early in the morning

until long into the evening

do they know I'm here

if they don't see my face

trying to keep up

trying to keep the pace

what if they start to wonder

what we do all day

because they don't see us

will they take our freedom away

BE THE GOOD

believe there is good in this world and you can find it everywhere you look

look past the division and hatred that breathes fire into the skies

the open desire to create discord and unrest so they hide

the hostility towards suffering in those you pass by

seek out the beauty and goodwill instead of

devastation. people are born to be loved.

it is not natural to desire such heavy

division. where has our soul gone?

we can join together and stop

the fight. see the beauty

joy and goodness win

the fight. see the beauty

we can join together and stop

division. where has our soul gone?

it is not natural to desire such heavy

devastation. people are born to be loved.

seek out the beauty and goodwill instead of

the hostility towards suffering in those you pass by

the open desire to create discord and unrest so they hide

look past the division and hatred that breathes fire into the skies

believe there is good in this world and you can find it everywhere you look

"PLEASE BROTHER"

originally published in "Their Footsteps: a collection of travel poems and photographs" sharing again to remind the world of the importance of ongoing devastation and starvation that is exasperated by government inaction during the Covid-19 Pandemic

"please brother"
his eyes are pleading
begging
as his wife pushes him forward
his wheelchair banging
against the bright orange rickshaw
where a stranger sits ignoring
the thin arms stretched for a coin
that never comes

"please brother"
the only request he knows
his legs lost just at the knee
he clings to his seat
and clutches his metal plate to his chest
his chair bouncing
against the broken pavement below

as they speed towards the line
to wait for their rations

"please brother"
he coughs from behind his scarf
pulled up to his nose
protecting his face
from the heavy clouds
of grime and dirt and smog
as it weighs down
against his frail shoulders
as heavy as the starvation

"please brother"
he whispers toward the fruit
his eyes barely able
to meet the gaze of the man standing
there behind the table
watching him wearily
the frail man thinks of his children
and raises his arms
imploring with the only words he can

"please brother"

SEPTEMBER

I FOLLOW

I follow in ruin;

prowling.

aching at the daylight.

I am conscious

of the roar

coursing through

my chest.

WHO HAS THE GUN

he was black

and shot in the back

seven times

for unknown crimes

bystanders said

the police were misled

the police claimed

they weren't to blame

protests were ready

nerves unsteady

again the same year

people living in fear

not allowed to fight

unless their skin is white

then you can shoot a gun

without having to run

like the kid named Kyle

who shot with a smile

but his skin was pale

so strangers paid his bail

I was recently told

that I was too bold

to say racism exists

and that I persist

to say we need to fight

to stand up for what's right

we've seen it straight

the world's in a state

but this man told me

that I just couldn't see

"racism was no longer here

there is nothing to fear"

even on the same day

that the bodies decay

of those killed unfairly

while others walk unwary

true, it's not as it was before

but you still can't ignore

that the racism is still here

minorities on a lower tier

before they even get a start

to see it, you need a heart

and eyes open wide

then, maybe you can no longer hide

I AM WOMAN

I am woman

hear me roar

I do not bow to you

my body is my own

not yours because

you can simply overpower

it with your anger

I have walk scared

around the corners of buildings

through the streets

in the night

knowing I could disappear

in only a moment

I have stayed quiet

against inequality

in pay

and respect

and voice

out of fear

of losing

the forward steps I have

gained

I have been called easy

a prude

slutty

cold

and that I should smile more

I was told that

feminism was a bad word

so that I fit into the mod

that woman should fit into

for that moment

seen and not heard

but it is no longer women

who should live in fear

and stay silent

we are strong

we are bold

we are smart

and if we stand together

hand in hand

across the world

then nothing can put us back

into the box where

we no longer belong

so, now stand with me

and shout,

"I am woman

hear me roar."

ON THE STREET

I saw a man crying

on the street today

I'm ashamed to say

that it took me a moment

to walk his way.

but honestly with covid

you just don't know if it's safe.

did I lose my humanity

replaced by cynicism and fear?

almost passing a man crying

instead of holding him dear.

I stopped and said "hello"

he look up at me

no mask on his face

but down to his side

tossed against the cement

"why are you crying mister?"

he shook his head and

bowed it down again

continuing to weep

I couldn't hug him close

or help him to his feet

because that would mean touching

and that's just way too deep

so instead I asked if he

needed anything from me

he shook his head and

looked again

giving me a small

smile while the tears

still flowed.

I walked away

not sure what to say

but knowing that he

was broken,

broke a piece of me

as well.

BUBBLING COLOR

bubbling

and bubbling

this expert glow

of true color

and well-being.

brilliant color

that does not define us

but rather builds us up

and makes us whole.

WE TRY

we try

we try

everyone tries to be stronger

better and brighter

because they don't see

the struggle so deep

in the eyes of those they meet

she can't breathe

the anxiety is so deep

pulling air between her teeth

hiding behind the mask she keeps

she's alone... or so it would seem

he worries about his mom

trying to keep her calm

talking through the intercom

and rubbing the germs from his palm

he's alone... or so it would seem

she feels like a failure

because she can't be a mother

and make her husband a father

like everyone around her

she's alone... or so it would seem

he can't leave his bed

since he piled up the dead

bodies, widespread

death without bloodshed

he's alone... or so it would seem

they can't make the rent

their money is all spent

it was never their intent

to sleep in a travel tent

they're alone... or so it would seem

the environment is toxic

and she is so homesick

but the world is sick

and there is no quick trick

she's alone... or so it would seem

we try

we try

everyone tries to be stronger

better and brighter

because they don't see

the struggle so deep

in the eyes of those they meet

I STAND HERE

I stand here

a testimony in stretch pants

that don't stretch quite so far..

I stand here

skin growing pale

with a lack of sunlight.

I stand here

a tiny person

in a tiny box

in a great big city

on a large piece of land

on a larger planet.

I watch the world.

moving

turning

I stand here

fires burn on the other side

of the windowpane.

on the other side

of the world.

people die and I testify

with a pencil in hand.

I fight...

with words.

I stretch my slippered toes

and look out the window at

tiny cars slowly sliding

through the narrow tunnel

that guides them underground.

why do they wait?

I stand here

blood boiling

wanting to scream

wanting to laugh

wanting to find a voice

and lift my fist.

I stand here

wanting the fear to end

to go outside

and feel the sun on my face

and the MARCH in my step.

my toes wiggle

ready to move

fingers caressing the windowpane.

I stand here.

THE CLAPPING STOPPED

our hands got tired

as we clapped louder

to drown out the noise

of desertion and division

our palms turned red

and our voices hoarse

screaming our thanks

each night

at seven.

months into the onslaught

from a disease

and from our neighbors

who didn't listen

or sacrifice the same.

we banged pots

and played music

and honked

and yelled

and then one day

I heard nothing

but distant cries

drifting away

on the wind

hopefully soon to be followed

by the disappearance of the disease

for the masses.

so I closed the window.

OCTOBER

THE SIX FEET SIDESTEP

we're still doing the dance

as we pass on the street

the six feet sidestep

with everyone you meet

left foot with a right foot cross

the movements are so neat

sliding over each other

as we slide across the concrete

sometimes you see someone you know

and instinct tells you to greet

you think of human interaction

and you feel a skip to your heartbeat

but the last minute you remember

and hastily make the retreat

with a little wave and shuffle

moving to the downbeat

sometimes i forget

when I'm rushing for a treat

at the local bodega

that is just down the street

someone walks too close

and I feel the defeat

turning back home

and dragging my feet

FALL LEAVES

fall leaves on a new house

covering it in gold

like a drape

over a plastic table.

it provides character

to a characterless mold.

life to a box

in between boxes

where people forget

the beige

in the crumpling

crinkling

crumbling

sea of bold

orange and gold.

WHAT WILL REMAIN

the anxiety develops

from inside my heart

blocking and choking the words

that I try to impart

on the world

desperately wanting to feel

wanting to know

there is value in what I deal;

in what I think

and the actions that I do.

that there will be an imprint

and that my life will matter to you.

not forgotten and discarded

like the trash tossed out.

I stand and wonder

"what is this life all about?"

smoking my cigarette down

to the final draw

as I stand out in the cold night,

my hands burning raw.

thinking that there is no place

I'd rather be

and trying to convince myself

of the truth in that decree.

hating the disability of my

own stubborn mind

as I try and fail

to prove that I haven't declined.

breathe deep and hold back

the morbid curiosity

of what my death wont bring

and neither will your atrocity

a legacy

in a world filled to the brim

with legacies.

each held dear for only their kin

for only a short time

as the death-watch ticks

closer to our own extension.

life as we know it, transfixed.

no more art.

passion and music gone

and with it our voice

and soul, foregone.

as we kill each other

and fight within our own minds

and with our perceived enemies

that we're told are not our kind

from the voices drifting

from above;

afraid of what lies

on the other side of love.

or after the smoke clears

and what will last.

will these words remain?

or will they be outcast

like that discarded

cigarette butt

as it blows away

while we keep our eyes shut?

BLOOD ON THE GREEN AND WHITE

for my dear friends in Nigeria, standing up for what is right

as darkness fell

the flags came out

passed from hand to hand

as the voices dimmed

to wait for the police

to break the peace

the whispered hope

that the flags

gripped tightly between

the fingers

would serve as a badge

of protection

as a voice reminded the

men and women

that a soldier can't

shoot them

simply for holding the flag

of the country they love.

three hours pass

as the protesters

sit

in peace

before the repeated blast

starts erupting in the street

those men and women

now laying on the ground

as others flee

in pain

and the flags

once proud in green and white

now splattered with red

all only due to

a stand against brutality

that should never have

come to pass

and the power in the wrong

hands of history

there is blood on the flag

for all days

and we cry with you

from the other side

of the world

THE FLY

oh, that fly

what a guy

the little spy

he could have just gone by

or landed on the tie

but he's not shy

he is, after all, a fly

I'm sure I heard the cry

of a faint testify

as he tried to preoccupy

and we all tried to magnify

and identify

and to verify

that it wasn't a misapply

but truly, it was a little fly

that landed softly on the dry

hair of the blinding white guy

as he diligently tried to deify

and pretended to glorify

or simply to oversimplify

not knowing that little spy

was sitting right above his eye

we still haven't been able to clarify

who was that little fly

was he truly our ally

or something a bit more sly

Jeff Goldblum did deny

"it was not I!

I have an alibi!"

A PUMPKIN SMILE

a pumpkin smile

carved with care

the season forgotten

no kids screaming

laughing down the street

collecting the candy

from the outstretched arms

of strangers lit from behind

the crackle of witches is only

a whispered giggle from behind

closed doors

as porch lights

stay dim

but the pumpkin is still there

waiting to be cut open

guts pulled out by the handful

and the smile carved with care

HEROES OVER SCREENS

POW

BAM

SPLAT

the heroes of the past

collected by the child

treasured in the pages

fighting the villains

and the nazis

while upholding the values

of america's past

some people want to go

back to a time

that never really existed

but the heroes evolved

and the villains did too

united against 'the man'

while they still fight

hand to hand.

once alone, reading folded page by flashlight.

now a community unified

joining together

from across the world,

from the safety of our own homes.

our imaginations expand.

our hope grows.

and we join to stand together

for the love of the heroes

and the villains

as they become interchangeable

and evolve past one dimension

we join the fight for what's right;

to defend the poor and downtrodden

the books evolved and matured

just as the child did...

into the woman she is today.

she stands and joins the fight

with the costumed characters

from the worn out pages

and their updated persons on the screen today

and the heroes who create them.

the villains she now fights

are the real villains

trying to destroy the world today

with the rhetoric full of hate

and the heart full of anger

spewing misinformation

to the masses

she faces the foe

and lifts her fists

her cape swirling in her shadow

POW

BAM

SPLAT

THE OBITUARY

"hello darkness"

she says with a smile

gone too soon

survived by her grown son.

he lives in Albuquerque

not able to come back to say goodbye

but she cares not

she's already gone

there wont be a funeral

the letters spell

her husband gone years before

fighting the war with his body

and then in his head

she stayed

living in her midtown apartment

alone

but surrounded by friends

she had a daughter once

but she's gone now too

it doesn't say how or why

but that they'll now embrace

in the afterlife

her son has a wife

and two small kids

they called her 'grammy'

she did fight hard

we knew she was a fighter

but she couldn't fight this

and here she is

gone too soon

in lieu of flowers

please give donations

not that she really cares

she is already gone

leaning her head into the shadows

and smiling into the deep

"hello darkness"

NOVEMBER

ELECTION DAY

shivering in the cold

on the New York city street

but still standing bold

refusing to be beat

it was a sight to behold

people refusing a seat

waiting to pass the threshold

and leave the concrete

the laws we must uphold

we wont be browbeat

not to be controlled

or told to take a backseat

we've been polled

and they continue to bleat

but here stands each household

joking and rather upbeat

ready to take hold

and vote for a defeat

so we'll stand here in the cold

on the New York city street

NOBODY WAS BORN ON SKID ROW

"nobody was born on skid row"

he told me

"you have to be on the skids"

my legs were numb from sleeping

on only a thin

blanket that covered the ground

through the night

clutching my bag to my chest

so it would be there...

hopefully...

when I woke up

I had no money

or hope

so I gathered with those of the same

the ground smelled like piss

from the man who slept beside me

we are the forgotten...

or the ones who wish to be

looked upon with disgust

but as I looked around me I saw more

the desperate

the downtrodden

the heavy-hearted

the scared

the lonely

the heartbroken

the shipwrecked

the homeless

many once had a home and a life

taken for a number of reasons

now sleeping in piss

and hoping not to get stabbed in the night

still more scared of the police

that could take them away

at any moment

unprovoked

but not to a better place

still more ashamed when the

drugs wear off and they realize

where they are

for just a moment

desperate for the high again

so they can go back to forgetting

the pain and sadness

as you walk by on the streets

and complain about the mess

or the smell;

just remember

"nobody is born on skid row"

BONE

body and mind ache

I enter the world daily

bowing to the weight

THE LEAF

he was born

only a short

while ago.

he started as a young sprout

all shiny and green

growing strong

with his brothers

in the summer heat

plans for his life

he made in his mind

to travel far and wide

and become empowered

to share with others

he listened to stories

of those below

and curled up to dream

of elephants

and waterfalls

and the magic to see.

then he grew older and bitter

and he thought

'there's not enough time'

the days passed quicker

and here he stayed with his kin

the harder he pushed

the longer he stayed

until the days grew colder and

he found himself alone

there's no time like the present

nothing holding him back now

he had nothing to pack

he was ready to go

he pushed off from his home.

the wind caught him and he knew

that this was his time

just before he fell to the ground

to join the dead and dying below.

THE FIRST SNOW

the snow falls cheerfully from the sky

as if telling us to ignore the mess that the year has brought

it drifts down and covers the grime

putting a blanket of clean over the pain that was before

cleaning the sidewalks and hiding the trash bags

watering the ground below to make room for the flowers in the spring

the white flakes whisper to me

'it will be alright- we can start over'

it clings to my gloves as I lift them to rub it against my face

asking to wash away my own grime from the past year

the year I hope to forget

as I learn to forgive

THE WORKOUT

I tried working out today

after I weighed my fat

the number across the display

made me feel like a rat

I knew I had eaten

more than my share

and I couldn't compete in

a fight with a bear

but I didn't realize

I had done so bad

or gone up at lease a size

since jeans were now a fad

I have to do something

before I get any larger

I started with jumping

then leapt like a charger

punching the air

like it was a foe

starting to swear

with each tiny blow

after almost ten minutes

I dropped to the couch

before pouring a guinness

and looking down at my pouch

promising another round tomorrow

before I get too large

and before I even know

it, I can't fit on a barge

DECEMBER

TEMPORARY HOME

she turns the corner

down the hallway

where she now lives.

years ago she barely remembers

staying in a hotel almost

identical to this one;

it might have been this one.

laughing and drinking and

walking up to their room late

locked in arm with her husband.

she waved the memory away

and shuffled down the hall

in her bare feet;

seeing a box outside another door

with a beer label

and nudging it with her toe

to see if any cans remained.

nothing.

she heard a thud on the

other side of the door

and scuttled away before

anyone came out of that room.

likely a threat

but she wasn't waiting around

to see if it were true.

she fumbled with the card.

now those were different

last time it was a key

a real metal key.

now they gave her this card

and expected her to know what to do with it.

she slid it in four times before the light

turned green

'enter' it blinked

and she did.

the room smelled of smoke

and beer

but at least her

assigned roommate

was passed out

and she wouldn't have to listen

to the screaming

during this night.

she slid the half full can

towards her on the night stand

before picking it up

and taking a drink

thinking

'this was not the life I thought

I would have'

but here she is

back at this hotel.

if only the memories

would stop

haunting

her.

WORDS

smoke is billowing

inside my little head

trying to form letters

into words with meaning

before they fall

through my body

and onto the page

words flowing

and glowing

and growing

into substance

full of protest

and pizazz

words that make creatures stop

in their tracks

and full grown men

weep unashamed

and unabashed

before the letters

turn back into smoke

and drift off the page

my arm stretches out...

hands clasped

on nothing

as the words

slip away from me

and out across the universe

searching for one

more discerning

and deserving

of their power

APPROPRIATION OR HATE

you appropriate their culture,

don't hesitate to eat their food

and drink sake by the tubful

acting like an idiot when you do

you wear a kimono for a robe

and watch anime too

you round up the pandas

and show them at the zoo

but now that you are told to hate

you call it the 'wuhan flu'

you jeer and jest and shout

I think you've lost a screw

but now it's getting scarier

for my friends with a tan hue

because this hatred is growing

for anyone not like you

SLEEP

as I lay me down to sleep

I wonder what my dreams will reap

recently they've been rather bleak

and I've fallen in so deep

that I've woken with a shriek

when a ghastly hand sweeps

coldly across my cheek

I close my eyes and try not to peak

across the room, I hear a creak

in the darkness I picture sheep

imagine them forced to leap

I don't notice I've drifted asleep

until a sheep opens her mouth to speak

but all that emerges is a sound so weak

it almost makes me weep

she's lost her voice, not a peep

maybe from all the critique

or feeling like a freak

or thinking the futures bleak

I hold her close and keep

reminding her that she's unique

and the world is at her feet

and of the mountains she will leap

and here I stay until the sun begins to creep

REMOTE CELEBRATIONS

celebrations with a sad heart;

families staying far apart

for the safety of the whole.

only the selfish look for a loophole.

we remember the years that came before

and pray and hope for many more.

so here we stay alone in our homes;

to the kitchen and back we continue to roam.

eating our own left-overs from the fridge.

oh, the pie, I suppose just a smidge.

and another smidge and just a smidge more

until I have trouble fitting through the door.

'cus when I'm sad I eat 'til I'm full

and this fridge has more than a spoonful

of the holiday meals that I made myself,

before shuffling over to the bookshelf.

to look through the photos of years past.

remembering the times, oh what a blast.

I comfort with the reminder this sacrifice

that we choose to pay is well worth the price.

because in just a year from this very day

we will celebrate all together and be able to say,

"we did what was right and stayed tight,

so merry christmas to all and to all a good night!"

LONG TERM

we stood shoulder to shoulder

and shouted even louder

"black lives matter"

six months ago

we took the time to grow

saw the path of the ammo

we changed our photos to black

formed our diverse wolf pack

we can't allow ourselves to slide back

It's so easy to stop fighting

when the world still needs righting

it feels like we've finished uniting

but the fight is just getting started

we can't go half-hearted

the path ahead is still uncharted

it's time to make change that lasts

so our children wont ask

why we are still repeating the past

Don't stop being the ally

vocalizing the war cry

until the need is satisfied

JANUARY

WAVES

division so thick I can taste it

    like a stew

        that my grandmother used to make

our hope is betrayed

    by bullets

        working through flesh and bone

he made the waves

    as he shouted

        and spit hatred into the air

we're spiraling into a deep dark hole

    with no option...

        but to lift our heads and climb

shake off those shoulders

    from the weight of the world

        letting it drop into the scorched earth

raise those worn out arms

    and stand ready to fight back the dark

        with light

WHO IS YOUR DRUMMER?

shouting

intelligent protest

against the injustices

after mixed-up worshipers

listen to the drum

without a beat

VACCINE

we're almost through the quarantine

waiting patiently for that vaccine

trusting the science to take hold

to stop killing people young and old

saying goodbye to many a friend

now we're so close to the end

ready to rush into the light

we're exhausted from this fight

I count the days to hug my dad

and see my parent's new pad

I can't believe it's been almost a year

living here in this personal fear

we've almost made it

in just an extra little bit

I'll be on the other side

with my arms open wide

FRESH SNOW

the white sparkled crunch

beneath my heavy boots

disrupting the silence of the day

untouched and undisturbed

by man or beast

as I am the first to take a step

producing the first marks

in the pristine surface

and feeling powerful and new

it's only frozen water,

and nothing more,

the whisper stirs deep in my mind

it questions, sarcastically,

why the power in an action

that anyone else can do?

I shush the whisper away

not letting it upset my day

and my feeling of accomplishment

in being the first step down

as my little foot makes its mark

deep in the fresh fallen snow.

PARK BENCH

he sits on a bench in the park

mask in hand, breathing that cold air

tossing crumbs to the pigeons. they

coo. calling their friends to come near

and enjoy the feast tossed to them

by the lonely man sitting there

missing the ones who left before

oh pigeons, you will never know

the sorrow of living too long

the man thinks before putting on

his mask and pushing up from the

bench to go back home down the street.

ASYLUM

one in ninety-seven

that's the number

of people who are

forcibly displaced

every year.

every year

men, women, children

forced from their home

fleeing on foot

fearing for their lives

and the lives of their

loved ones

one in ninety-seven

displaced

hungry

beat down mentally

and physically

hoping for safety

and bravery

crawling towards a place

that is supposed to be

"better"

one in ninety-seven

and it will increase

as the population does

and the food decreases

with the water

more devastation

caused by nature

and man

and people flee.

one in ninety-seven

sitting on a boat

in the middle of the ocean

praying it doesn't sink

before they can reach

a safe border

where they aren't

being gunned down

in the streets

trying to not

drink the water

to quench their thirst.

one in ninety-seven

walking towards a wall

praying it doesn't stay closed

so they can come

and work

to make a living

to put food on the table

for their children

coming from a place

where the food is gone

a woman clutching

her child to her breast

not knowing he'll get taken

in the place she was told was safe.

one in ninety-seven

MARS

I want to be a rocket-man

and make my way to mars

it looks nice and peaceful

i think I could open a bar

maybe there will be no discord

or at least it will take a while

since I'd leave the people behind

and happily live my life exiled

FOLLOW THE BLIND

what inspiration made you think that it was ok?

to break into a building that wasn't yours

to threaten the people who we elected

to shout and yell and chase up the stairs.

the never-ending cycle of darwinism

that shows as each rubber sole climbs a new step

or shatters a new window of the building we share.

what inspired you to think that it was ok?

to go around a barricade

to refuse to wear a mask

to dispute racism as if it were fiction

to scream and shout about the "china virus."

what inspired you to think that there are pedophilia rings

heralded over by some of the people you used to support?

there are things you now scream; that are so far-fetched

there is no logical response.

did the world turn it's back on you when you couldn't get

your hair cut?

is that why you are so angry?

it can't be because you are being hunted in your own neighborhood

or because your children can't get the same education as the

ones down the street

or because you fear for your life when you leave your home

or worship your god

so who inspired you to be so afraid?

FEBRUARY

ANOTHER DAY

there's a dawning light

peaking over the buildings

as I make my breakfast

of scrambled eggs

and pour a whiskey

into a tumbler.

the light represents

hope for tomorrow

or maybe today

I take a sip

the cool liquid

burning as it goes down

the eggs brown

the sun comes up

again

WE DESERVE

we deserve
to not fear
what lies around
the corner
as we walk alone
our heels tapping
against the pavement
sidestepping the shadows
folding our limbs
tight against our
easily damaged body
told to be careful
justified in trepidation
that it is solely
our responsibility
or our fault
when it goes wrong

bullshit, I say
we deserve
to not fear.
we deserve
to be safe

हम हक़दार हैं translated to Hindi by Pankhuri Sinha

हम हक़दार हैं
एक सुरक्षित दुनिया के
इतना तो होना ही चाहिए
कि हमें मिले एक बेखौफ़ दुनिया!
ये हमारी अपेक्षाएँ हैं
और हम बिल्कुल इस
लायक कि हमें डरना न पड़े
कि जाने क्या छिपा है
कौन सा खतरा, अगले मोड़ पर!
कोने में, जब हम चलते हैं अकेले!
हमारे जूतों की एडियां
खनकती हैं फुटपाथ पर
छायाओं से आगे बढ़ती
समेटती अपनी बाहें, अपनी देह
अपने भीतर , हमारी उस देह के भीतर, जो नष्ट हो जाती है
कितनी आसानी से!
जिसे लगातार कहा जाता है
सावधान रहने के लिए!
एक अशांत घबराहट में ही
जिसे मिलता है जैसे न्याय
क्योंकि हमारी होती है
ज़िम्मेदारी, केवल हमारी गलती
अगर घटती है कोई दुर्घटना!

बकवास, कहती हूँ मैं
हमारी अपेक्षायें हैं और
हम उनके लायक भी
कि निडर जिएं !
और इतना तो हमें
मिलना ही चाहिए कि
हम महसूस करें सुरक्षित!

WE ARE HERE

I'm scared to go outside.

and don't try to persuade me that

it's rare I'll catch the virus.

because, when I take a deeper look

the virus is everywhere.

even if

many people follow the guidelines

people are still dying.

it's not true that

I can agree

because

we can be safe and healthy

if we all just work together

everyone just doesn't care.

I'm sure you can't tell me

it is safe out there..

(now read in reverse)

RBG

she drew the line in the sand

with her sword drawn she stands

ready to fight the foe

that we didn't even yet know

in one small body, the power

refusing to ever cower

making changes for generations to come

not allowing us to grow numb

it's time for us to carry the flame

stand up tall and exclaim

"we will never back down"

as her spirit is still around

it lives in the heart of us all

we only need to answer the call

THE MEMOIR OF AN INVISIBLE MAN

he was here

but now he's not.

a living man;

now barely a thought

from a bygone era

that we've almost forgot.

as we zoom along

he's in our blind spot.

did he make a difference

many years ago?

I can't remember.

maybe we'll never know

he might have flown high

mimicking a crow,

but the sun blinded us

with her bright glow.

now he's faded away;

a summer snowman.

or an old newspaper

chucked in the can.

fading into obscurity.

that wasn't the plan

or the thoughts and dreams

of the cellophane man.

HOLES

where people used to stand

now holes in the land

one for each soul moved on

maybe to a great beyond

voices silenced for good

life ended before it should

now holes in the land

as we reach out our hand

trying to hold to the breath

that left you with your death

never to come again

it's over before it began

they said it wasn't their fault

as they killed you without assault

refusing to give a shit

or even to really admit

that they weren't a hypocrite

or lacking the wit

to know enough to not commit

that wearing just a bit of knit

is wasn't showing a submit

it was to stop the transmit

of a virus that continues to span

creating holes across the land

WHAT NEXT

Well here we are – well into 2021. And even with two parts, I managed to only cover a small portion of what has happened in NYC in 2020, let alone throughout the US or the world. But I'm sharing my moments. The ones I felt, I recognized, or I shared with people I know and love. All moments are just as powerful to those who experience them.

At this point in our lives – and in the world – there is so much going on that we cannot control. We cannot know how items are impacting others, mentally and physically, but what we can do is to come together for love and equality and health – for each other and for the greater good that is humanity.

Empathy will get us all a long way.

And for what you can do for the future of humanity:
- Educate yourself by multiple / unbiased sources
- Treat others fairly
- Do not prematurely judge
- Do your part to help others
- Get vaccinated
- Fight for what is right
- Realize others have it worse
- Understand the truth about your privilege
- Be Kind
- continue to vote on local and broader subjects!

A portion of the sales of this book will donated to "Color Of Change." An organization that helps place decision-makers in corporations and government to create a more human and less hostile world for black people in America

A portion of the sales of this book will be donated to "Coalition for The Homeless." This organization is especially important right now as the homeless population continues to suffer through the impacts of Covid-19 and will continue to grow with many impending evictions.